Critical Thinking Skills Workbook

Questions, Exercises and Games to Develop Your Problem Solving, Critical Thinking and Goal Achieving Skills

Table of Contents

Introduction

There's a saying that "as a man thinketh, so is he." I believe that's right. That's why to succeed in life; we must know how to think the right way. And by the right way, I mean think critically.

Critical thinking is at the core of every successful person in the history of the world. That's why all of us need to develop our critical thinking skills.

This book is about helping you develop your critical thinking skills so that you can be the best learner you can be and the most effective problem solver you can be. When you become those, your chances of becoming successful in life aren't far behind.

So if you're ready to develop your critical thinking skills for personal success, turn the page and let's begin!

Go To - http://bit.ly/CompleteConcentration

Chapter 1 - The What's and Why's of Critical Thinking

Contrary to how it may sound, critical thinking isn't about being a pessimist, negative thinker, or someone who is critical of people and things. According to what's probably the single best authority on critical thinking, which is The Foundation for Critical Thinking, critical thinking can be defined as a process that's disciplined intellectually, which involves the skillful and active evaluation, synthesizing, analyzing, applying and conceptualizing of information that's generated by or gathered from various sources such as communications, reasoning, reflection experience or observation. Further, information gathered or generated from such sources can be used as guides for one's belief and actions.

If that sounds rather geeky, nerdy or technical, let me break it down for you in simpler terms: critical thinking refers to a systematic and deliberate way of processing information in order to better understand things and, in the process, make much better or wiser decisions. Now you may think, why did I have to include the very technical definition from the Foundation for Critical Thinking? It's because the rather wordy definition they gave identifies the different ways by which you can process information as well as the various possible sources of such information.

So what constitutes critical thinking skills? These include:

- Ability to analyze;
- Ability to apply standards;
- Ability to ask thoughtful questions;
- Ability to assess things;
- Clarifying unclear things;
- Cognitive Flexibility
- Ability to communicate;
- Ability to conceptualize;
- Creativity;
- Curiosity;
- Ability to make decisions;
- Ability to embrace different cultural perspectives;
- Ability to evaluate things;
- Ability to explain things clearly;
- Ability to think or look ahead, i.e., foresight;
- Ability to identify patterns;
- Imagination;
- Ability to seek information in the right places;
- Ability to interpret;
- Ability to make sound but not necessarily perfect judgments;
- Ability to reason logically;
- Ability to make abstract connections;
- Ability to infer from available information;
- Objectivity;
- Ability or habit of observing things;
- Thinking open-mindedly;
- Ability to make rational predictions;
- Ability to present clearly;
- Ability to solve problems;
- Questioning arguments or evidences presented;
- Ability to reason well;
- Ability to recognize similarities and differences;

- Ability to reflect;
- Skepticism;
- Ability to synthesize information and things learned;

Of these critical thinking skills, 5 are considered as most crucial. These are:

- **Analytical**: This refers to the skill of being able to examine information, know what it means, and what symbolizes or exemplifies.
- **Communication**: This refers to the ability to clearly express or relay to others what you understand, i.e., your ideas, thoughts, and arguments. This is important especially if you're working with other people and need their support or assistance to get things done.
- **Creativity**: This refers to the ability to identify specific patterns in information presented to you that most others aren't able to see and, in the process, create solutions or approaches that nobody else is able to. In essence, this is the ability to see things - not as they obviously are - but what they are on a deeper level and the ability to act accordingly.
- **Open-Mindedness**: This refers to the ability to temporarily set aside any biases or pre-conceived notions about an idea or information presented to be able to objectively assess its merits or demerits. Biases and pre-conceived notions result in the inability to correctly see an idea's merits and demerits and consequently, compromises one's ability to take the best possible action on the said information.
- **Problem Solving**: This refers to the ability to not just analyze problems and coming up with

the best possible solutions but also to implement those solutions effectively.

Why should you seriously think about critical thinking? Is it that important? Yes, it is! When you think about it, most of what we think on a daily basis is uncritical or doesn't go through serious evaluation or thinking. Now that itself isn't bad. In fact, uncritical thinking is also crucial to living a normal and productive life. Why?

If you had to evaluate and think about every single thing you do every day, what do you think would happen? What if you had to always deliberate about whether or not you'd wake up to go to work, if you should brush your teeth before leaving the house, or if you should wear a round neck shirt or a dress shirt to work, among so many other trivial things? Do you think you'd have enough energy to think about the more serious stuff like your work responsibilities, whether or the crucial details of the financial analysis reports you prepare for the deliberation of your company's board of directors, or if you should give your seriously ill patient this medicine or that medicine? Further, do you think 24 hours would be enough time for you to get everything you need to do done by the end of the day? No way! So what's the problem with uncritical thinking for the most part?

Well, it becomes a concern when - because most of our daily thinking is uncritical or automatic - we apply uncritical thinking to the things that really matter, like where to invest our hard-earned money in preparation for our retirement, whether or not to buy a house in Long Island or in Beverly Hills, or if you should quit your current job to switch to a potentially more lucrative (and profitable) career. Because most of the things we need to decide on every day only require minimal thinking or processing, the possibility of under-utilizing our minds is very high. And if we don't exercise our minds primarily through the practice of serious or critical thinking, we run the risk of mind atrophy, i.e., a weakened mind that's incapable of much serious and deeper evaluation and processing of information to guide us into making very important decisions. And there are several different ways in which critical thinking can be critical for our personal success.

As A Student

As a student, critical thinking can spell the difference between graduating with honors and not graduating at all. Why? Students are at high risk of acquiring wrong attitudes about very hard questions or problems. According to the author of The Thinking Student's Guide to College, Andrew Roberts, some of these wrong attitudes include:

- **Ignorant Certainty**: This refers to a person's belief that all questions have a fixed number of correct answers and that all a person needs to do to be able to answer questions is to know where to look for the answers. For example, the multiplication table. The equation 5 x 5 only has 1 definite answer, which is 25. And students learn the right answer through a multiplication table provided by their teachers or their schools. Many students, especially those who have just set foot on universities, think that this way of answering questions in school is enough to get them by both in school and in life. But they often find that as their stints in universities or colleges progress, the most meaningful and challenging questions both in school and in life aren't as simple and straightforward as they were in high school. In order to successfully finish college, students need to be able to think critically about the stuff they're required to study. And in the real world, being able to think critically is what can spell the difference between striving and thriving in life.

— **Naive Relativism**: This attitude is one where students think that all things are relative, i.e., all answers to life's - and school's - questions are equal and that there are no singular truths or right answers. This attitude is adopted by students usually after they've been enlightened on the errors of ignorant certainty. And when you compare naive relativism to ignorant certainty, it's certainly the more "critical thinking-like" attitude because it isn't narrow and it requires a bit more thought. But it doesn't mean it's the right attitude. Why? It's because it completely misses the point of critical thinking, which is to arrive at the best possible answer to questions. Critical thinking involves being able to determine whether or not your reasoning or arguments, as well as those of other people's, are valid or not. That's why in order to think critically, people should accept the fact that all answers aren't equal and that more often than not, some are much better than others or some are right while others are wrong.

Critical thinking allows students to avoid the pitfalls of the above-mentioned attitudes towards learning and answering questions and consequently, successfully graduate from school by:

- Allowing them to form their own views and understand their learning material on a much deeper level, which is key to engaging in intelligent discussions with teachers and schoolmates, as well as in writing great essays.
- Enabling them to come up with logical and irrefutable arguments for their positions. This is even more crucial for Masters or Doctorate students, where original and critical thinking are absolutely required.
- Helping them to properly critique or appraise their own works, which almost always leads to much higher grades and much better thinking habits.

In other words, going through school - especially college or university - without the ability to think critically is pretty much like walking in the dark, i.e., you'll definitely get somewhere, though it's probably not where you really want to go. And even after school, when students venture out into the real world, critical thinking still matters. In fact, it may even matter more after school! Why?

- Critical thinking helps continuous intellectual growth and learning, which need not stop after formal schooling. Learning is a lifetime endeavor because as people age, they continue to come across different new pieces of information. If the ability to think critically isn't there, chances are high that a person won't be able to properly process them and fail to make the most out of them.
- Critical thinking helps in decision making, especially on matters that can be very difficult

to decide on. The ability to think this way can help people identify all possible alternatives or options, and weigh the advantages and disadvantages of all possible alternatives or options to make the wisest decisions possible.

- Critical thinking can help in defending against scammers, con men and manipulators. When a person never thinks deeper than what's obvious from the surface and always takes things at face value, they run the very high risk of attracting and being victimized by dubious characters who have nothing but evil intentions. Consider many of the advertisements for weight loss. While it's an established scientific fact that crash diets aren't healthy and aren't effective in keeping the weight off, many people still get duped into purchasing products that promise "lose 10 pounds in a week" or "lose 50 pounds without diet or exercise." Why? Because these people never made it a habit to think critically, i.e., question the claims and promises of these hucksters.
- Critical thinking helps make people high employable and pirate-able. People who have excellent critical thinking skills tend to be very good problem solvers or solution makers, which are very in demand in just about any company or organization.

And speaking of after graduation from university or college...

Critical Thinking and Employment

The ability to think critically is definitely a very precious commodity in the labor market, one which gives any person possessing them a distinct edge - and a higher pay offer - than people who don't have it. As mentioned earlier, being able to think critically can help any person make very wise and effective decisions through the ability to objectively and optimally analyze any and all available information.

Thinking critically requires that a person be able to carefully and wisely evaluate information, facts, data, research findings and observable phenomenon. People who think critically are able to come up with logical conclusions from available information as well as to distinguish useful information from useless ones in terms of making specific decisions.

However you look at it, critical thinking is essential to succeed in just about any career in any industry. People want to hire applicants who can analyze situations via logical thinking and can think of solutions that really work. A person who has very good critical thinking skills is someone that doesn't need any micromanaging or hand-holding because he or she can be trusted to make sound decisions on his or her own.

If you're currently in the job-hunting market, how can you showcase your critical thinking skills while applying for the jobs you really want? You can do this by being able to properly communicate to your prospective employer your top critical thinking skills, which is among the ones we enumerated earlier. And how do you do this?

One way is to emphasize your specific critical thinking skills all throughout your job-searching efforts, especially if critical thinking is an implied or stated qualification for the jobs you're applying for. You can do this by:

- Include the phrase "critical thinking" or "critical thinking skills" and other relevant terms in your resume, more specifically in the relevant work history sections and also in your resume's summary section, if included.
- In your resume or application's cover letter, you can mention a critical thinking skill or two within the letter's body. And don't forget to mention particular examples or instances when those critical thinking skills were put to good use at work.
- And during your interviews, look out for opportunities to mention or "humble brag" your critical thinking skills by citing work examples where you were able to use those skills.

Chapter 2 - Developing Your Critical Thinking Skills

Now that you know what critical thinking skills are and why they're important, it's time to get to the meat of this book: how you can develop your critical thinking skills. In this chapter, we'll take a look at the general ways you can do this. In the succeeding chapters, we'll take a look at more detailed or focused means by which you can become the best critical thinker you can be.

Ask

There are times that explanations can turn into the most complicated and complex answers that make people even more confused or perplexed. One way to minimize this risk is to continually ask yourself questions, the most basic ones that you did at the time you started solving problems or mysteries. If this sounds a bit unclear to you, you can ask yourself questions such as the following in order to analyze problems better and in the process, solve them:
- What do I already know about this problem?
- How do I know it?
- What is it that I'm trying to evaluate, show, prove, or disprove about this problem, statement or argument?
- Is there something I'm missing or overlooking here?

You'd be surprised at the power of even the simplest questions that get asked repeatedly. To be able to solve complex problems, work on their simpler aspects first. And one of the best ways to do that is by asking simple questions first.

Don't Just Assume

There's a saying that assumptions make an ass out of everybody in a conversation. I don't think it holds true all the time. I think it holds true especially when a problem is being solved. It's very easy to make a fool of yourself as you attempt to solve challenging problems by simply assuming things without the benefit of questioning such assumptions. When you look at the world's greatest critical thinkers who have made our world a much better place compared to centuries ago like Einstein, Newton and even Steve Jobs, you will see people who have challenged people's basic assumptions that maintained the status quos in the past. Major breakthroughs, solutions, and innovations don't come by accepting the status quo and their underlying assumptions.

Think About How You Think

The human brain, which is more powerful or complex than any of the world's most powerful computers, is certainly an amazing thing to behold. However, the speed at which it can process information can at times be disadvantageous, especially when it's done during times where critical thinking is needed.

Part of the human brain's amazing capabilities is using heuristics or mental shortcuts to make sense of the information it receives and the things that are going on all around. This was definitely a huge advantage back in the days when man had to consistently kill for food or be killed by his food in the wild. But this way of making sense of things can be very disadvantageous when applied to things that require critical thinking such as whom to marry, vote for president, or hire as a babysitter.

Critical thinkers are cognizant of their own mental or thought process biases as well as their own prejudices and how their decisions and courses of actions can be influenced by these biases and prejudices. You should be too if you want to develop your critical thinking skills.

Reverse Engineer Stuff

It's very frustrating to be stuck on a very sticky problem or stubborn situation, despite all the hard work and critical thinking you've put in. One way to break the impasse is to reverse engineer your problem or situation, i.e., think in reverse. For example, "it seems evident that my sluggishness is keeping me obese. Could it be possible that my obesity is causing my sluggishness?"

Reverse thinking isn't a guarantee because you don't always get things in reverse when trying to solve problems. However, a major benefit to thinking in reverse is the very good possibility of opening your mind to alternative solutions that may actually work. Hence, reverse thinking can be a very good tactic for getting out of a rut when solving a problem.

Check the Current Evidence

When you're trying to solve a problem, it's worth keeping in mind that you don't have to reinvent the wheel. If a wheel has already been created for that type of challenge, then, by all means, use it! Of if it's not exactly the kind of wheel that'll completely solve your problem, then consider building on that wheel instead of trying to reconstruct that wheel into something even more. Get it?

But before you rush to use the same approach that others before you have already used, you must first evaluate the solution or approach, i.e., the problem it solved is generally the same as the one you're trying to solve and that the circumstances surrounding both aren't too far off. It's possible that on the surface, the problems and their underlying circumstances look to be the same, which can lead you to quickly assume that such is the case and immediately apply the same approach or solution to solving your problem. But what if upon closer inspection and evaluation, they're not as similar as you thought? Then you'll probably bang your head against the wall, regretting that you didn't evaluate further first.

So how can you evaluate an existing or similar solution to determine whether or not it's something you can apply to your own situation? By asking yourself the following questions on any information or evidence presented to you or you encounter:
  - Who collected this information or evidence?
  - How was this collected or obtained?
  - Why, or what was the motive behind the information or evidence?

To be more specific, let's take the case for a study showing the health benefits of eating an abundant amount of beef and pork on a regular basis. When you check the supporting studies, they look very convincing. Until you find out that the people who funded the study were, surprise surprise, the American Association of Meat! And while that fact doesn't necessarily render the actual results of the study worthless or untruthful, it should give you a good enough reason to not just accept the evidence and instead, dig deeper.

Don't Outsource Your Thinking Process

Sometimes, it can be very tempting to just think the thoughts of others when doing very tedious and meticulous research. Simply accepting the thinking rationale and ideas of the information you've researched - especially if they're favorable to or supports your ideas and positions - is a very attractive proposition when you're already tired and at the end of your rope. But you should always accept the ideas of or information from others only after you've evaluated them to be reliable or trustworthy. Don't just assume that because the people behind those ideas and information are well-regarded and well-respected, they're always correct or that their ideas are the best ones for the challenge you're trying to solve. If you make that a habit, you become less and less of a critical thinker and your risks for making more serious wrong decisions becomes much higher.

Critical Thinking Isn't a 7-Eleven

Lastly, you can develop your critical thinking skills by, paradoxically, not practicing it all the time. Just because it's a crucial skill to have doesn't mean you should practice it 24/7! Most of the things you need to act or decide on do not need to the critical thinking process. What toothpaste should I buy? Which shirt should I wear to the grocery today? Should I watch Game of Thrones or Walking Dead? No, you don't need to research and do a SWOT analysis just to be able to decide on things like these. Give yourself a break! Save it for when it's really needed. Just don't forget to practice using it regularly, which is entirely different from using it all the time!

Chapter 3 - How to Ask Questions that Promote Critical Thinking

It can be very tempting to assume that answers, at least direct ones, are the only answers to questions, challenges and problems encountered. But many are the instances when no direct answers are visible on the horizon. During such moments, the best answers to your questions are, paradoxically, questions.

Asking the right questions can help you discover the answers and solutions you need. This is because asking more questions can help you discover roads or routes that can lead you to answers that aren't as obvious at the beginning.

The Right Type of Questions

But you shouldn't just ask any type of questions. You must avoid asking questions that are merely answerable by a yes, no, or just by one or two words. In other words, you must minimize asking close-ended questions, i.e., questions that have 1-dimensional replies, and ask open-ended questions instead. Closed-ended questions usually begin with "what," "when," and "who." On the other hand, open-ended ones usually begin with "how" and "why."

It's been said that failing to plan is planning to fail. It's certainly the case with asking questions that can help you develop your critical thinking skills even more. And to help you plan your questions well, you can make use of what's called as Bloom's Taxonomy to determine whether or not something is worth probing deeper or if you need to employ a higher level of thinking on it. The following are Bloom's updated Taxonomy of Cognitive processes from lowest to highest:

- Knowledge: This refers to your ability to recall concepts, opinions, and facts.
- Comprehension: This refers to your ability to understand, organize and express information in your own words and not just verbatim or memorized.
- Application: This pertains to your ability to use what you learned in a relatively new situation.
- Analysis: This pertains to your ability to establish relationships among variables in the information presented to you or you've gathered.
- Evaluation: This is your ability to make use of standards and criteria to make decisions or judgments.
- Creation or Synthesis: This refers to your ability to combine together facts and information into one consistent solution, idea, or argument, as well as the ability to use your creativity to understand things better by relating different pieces of information to each other.

To give you a clearer picture of how to ask questions that can help you become better at critical thinking, here are example so such questions per item in Bloom's Taxonomy.

Knowledge
- What is/are _______?
- When did you _______?

- How would you elaborate on______?
- What's the reason for ___________?
- How would you depict or portray ___________?

Comprehension
- How would you differentiate _______ from ________?
- In your own words, can you explain ___________?
- What ideas or characteristics show that ________?
- What proof is there that ________?

Application
- What illustration can you give to show that ________?
- How would you demonstrate your understanding of _______?
- To do or demonstrate this, what approach would you utilize?
- If ________, what do you think would've happened?

Analysis
- What can you infer from this?
- How would you group these?
- How would you label this?
- What unique traits differentiate this from the others?

Evaluation
- How can you compare ______ with _______?
- Of the options available, which is better?
- When it comes to _______, why is ________ important?

- What would you have recommended?

Creation/Synthesis
- If __________, what could've happened?
- What could be an alternative way to interpret __________?
- How can this be solved?

Critical Thinking Questions for Studying or Learning

When you are trying to study or learn something, it's impossible to do it well without the ability to think critically. What is critical thinking within the context of studying or learning something? Terry Heick, the author of What Does Critical Thinking Mean, says that critical thinking is all about looking at that which you're trying to learn from all possible sides or angles, the purpose of which is to understand it in a way that's exclusive to you, i.e., in a very personal way. Critical thinking in the context of studying or learning also means seeing the different parts, functions, contexts, and forms of that which you're trying to learn or study.

After you've looked and analyzed the thing you're learning or studying from different sides, angles, and contexts, you'll be in a very good position to evaluate or judge it based on your own unique way of thinking about that thing. The goal of doing so is to be able to see the merits and demerits, as well as biases or objective points so you can arrive at a conclusion or perspective that's yours and not just pirated from somebody else. And when you're able to generate your own conclusions or perspectives about those which you're studying or learning, you'll be able to get an intimate understanding of it, which is the goal of studying or learning.

To think critically about something for the purpose of learning or coming up with the best solutions, we've talked about the importance of asking the right questions. In this part of the chapter, we'll take a look at specific critical thinking questions that can help you learn any material or content much deeper and better. And to be more specific, we'll take a look at 48 critical thinking questions from globaldigitalcitizen.org that you can ask yourself to help you understand any learning material much better. Ask yourself these questions about the material you're learning or studying to get a deeper understanding of the material.

1. Who will benefit from this material/information?
2. Who else have you heard talk about this material/information?
3. Who are the people that are most affected by this information?
4. To whom is this material/information least beneficial to?
5. Who'd be the best person I know to ask about this?
6. Who decides on this type of information?
7. Who are the key people?
8. Who deserves credit for this information?
9. What are the identifiable weaknesses/strengths in this piece of information/material?
10. What are the worst and best case scenarios in the material?
11. What other perspectives are worth looking into in this material?

12. What are the most and least critical points of the material?
13. What are the alternative points or ideas concerning the information in the material?
14. What else can I do to positively add to or change this material?
15. What could be a good counter-argument for the points presented here that I'm not agreeable to?
16. What are hindrances to my being able to act on the information presented in the material?
17. Where can I see these ideas applied in real life?
18. Where can I obtain additional information?
19. Where can I find similar or related situations or concepts?
20. Where can I get assistance in terms of understanding the material further?
21. Where is this information or material needed most?
22. Where will the information presented in the material take me?
23. Where in my life would the information presented in the material be challenging or problematic?
24. Where can I improve myself based on the information presented?
25. When will the ideas or information in the material be considered valid or invalid?
26. When will I know if I've succeeded based on the information in the material?
27. When can the material benefit me or my family?
28. When has the information presented here played - if at all - played an important role in my life or in world history?

29. When could the information be considered problematic?
30. When can I expect things to change based on the information?
31. When's the optimal time to apply the ideas presented in the material?
32. When should I turn to others for help when it comes to applying or understanding the ideas presented in the material?
33. If there's a challenge or problem presented in the material, why would that be so?
34. Why must I or other people understand the ideas presented here?
35. Why are the ideas in the material important or relevant to me and to others?
36. Why has the situation portrayed in the material persisted for a long time?
37. Why are the scenarios presented in the material considered to be the best and worst case ones?
38. Why did the situation presented in the material come to pass and continue to persist?
39. Why do people believe the points or ideas presented here?
40. Why do I and other people need to understand the ideas presented in the material?
41. How are the ideas presented here similar to others?
42. How do these ideas or information benefit me and other people?
43. How do the ideas and information presented in the material disrupt the status quo?
44. How can the ideas and information presented in the material harm me and other people?
45. How can I know whether or not these ideas are valid or not, true or false?

46. How do I see these ideas changing the way things are done in the future?
47. How can I safely apply the ideas and information from this material?
48. How can I use these ideas and information for my and other people's benefit?

General Questions for Developing Critical Thinking for Any Situation

Asking yourself these 6 questions can help you become much better at thinking critically and become a more effective problem solver.

- What's going on?
- What's the significance or importance of this?
- Is there something else I need to see or know about the situation that can help me better address or deal with it?
- How did I come to this specific conclusion or knowledge about the situation?
- If other people are involved, who are they and what's their stand on a specific issue in the situation? How can their identity and their stand possibly affect the way they think about the situation?
- What else do I need to consider and how can it help me better address the situation?

Download Your Free EBook – Complete Concentration

Go To - http://bit.ly/CompleteConcentration

Chapter 4 - Mental Exercises to Develop Your Critical Thinking Skills

Another way you can develop your critical thinking skills is by performing mental exercises on a regular basis. Why? The mind is practically a mental "muscle," and just like your physical muscles, your mind's ability to perform will largely depend on whether or not you subject it to regular and purposeful training. In this chapter, we'll take a look at some of the best mental exercises to perform regularly to make your mind more and more adept at this skill called critical thinking.

Take note that you don't have to perform all of them in one sitting. You only need to do a couple of them regularly, and you can mix it up every now and then. The important thing is you challenge your mind continuously to grow.

Read Books

One way to start becoming a much better critical thinker is to expose yourself to different ideas from different thought leaders. You can watch their videos or read their books. Personally, I believe reading books is a much better option. Why?

It's because with their ideas written in print, it's much easier to highlight and take notes and revert to them when needed. Plus, you don't need a smartphone or a computer just to be able to access these thought leaders' ideas. With a book, physical or electronic, you can easily go back to ideas you've already read via bookmarks and highlights, and you can also take your time reflecting on them because books don't move, unlike videos.

The best way to read through a book, especially relatively long and thick ones, is the same way you should eat an elephant: one bite at a time. When it comes to reading, make it your goal to read a thought-provoking one from a well-known thought leader such as Simon Sinek, Malcolm Gladwell and Thomas Friedman among others, by reading one chapter daily or for at least 30 minutes every day. That way, it can become an automatic action, i.e., a habit that you'll no longer have to think about doing.

Study Other People

Some of the most beneficial people to study are those that have accomplished the things you're looking to do yourself and business or career competitors if you have any. Why? Studying people who have already accomplished things you're aiming to do will help you cut your learning curve by among other things, helping you see how things can be done or how problems can be addressed from a different perspective. As Albert Einstein once said: No problem can be solved from the same level of consciousness that created it. By studying those who have gone before you, it's possible to achieve a higher level of consciousness or thinking about your most elusive goals.

And what about your competitors? Studying them can also help you see things from a different perspective, that of a defensive one. If they're you're competitors; it means they're a threat to you in terms of business or your career at the office. When you study them, particularly how they think, the way they live their lives, their motivations and their personalities, you can ask yourself better questions concerning how you can avoid being outperformed by them. By getting into their heads and thinking the way they think as best as you can, you can increase your chances of consistently outperforming them and staying on top of your game.

Adopt a Problem

No, I'm not talking about adopting a problem child. I really meant to suggest adopting a problem, i.e., a problem you don't have, but other people do. Now you may be wondering why on earth you should burden yourself with a problem that isn't yours.

Hold on for a minute there, Sparky! What I mean by adopting a problem is this: look for a problem that others are currently encountering and try to analyze that problem to come up with a theoretical solution. That's it! You don't have to shoulder the burden of solving other people's problems, but you can become even better at critical thinking by analyzing other people's problems that can be applicable to your situation under a different set of circumstances. Another benefit of this exercise is if the time comes you encounter something similar; you already have an idea of how to solve it!

Dear Diary

Alright, that sounds a bit cheesy or childish. Allow me to rephrase it: journal every day. There are several critical thinking benefits you can enjoy from doing so.

First, journaling may be considered a keystone habit, i.e., a habit that once changed can lead to changes in other habits without much effort. It's like hitting multiple birds with just one rock.

Another benefit to journaling your daily experiences, thoughts, experiences, successes, and failures is that you start becoming more and more aware of the things that are happening to and around you. Things that impact your ability to succeed or fail in your endeavors. And with increased awareness comes an increased ability to analyze situations and come up with much better solutions.

Lastly, journaling is one of the best ways to process information that you receive and create throughout the day, which is crucial for effective learning and problem solving. There's something about writing down information and how you think and feel about them on paper or typing them on a digital journal that makes you understand them much better.

Bubble Gum

Yes, bubble gum can help you develop your critical thinking skills! By what mechanism, I don't know exactly. But dig this - research conducted by Kate Morgan and her colleagues that was published in the British Journal of Psychology in 2013 found that chewing gum can help briefly improve memory, focus and concentration. And this isn't the only study that validates the idea that chewing gum helps improve cognitive function - there are many others like it!

Critical thinking requires a great deal of focus and concentration. Since chewing gum helps improve such abilities, however brief, it can help you develop your critical thinking skills. Just stick to sugar-free gums to avoid "crashing down," which is usually the case when consuming sugar-filled foods and drinks.

Play Mind Games

As mentioned earlier, your mind is like your physical muscles in the sense that if you don't use it regularly, it atrophies or becomes weaker over time. That's why I'm emphasizing the importance of regularly engaging your mind in mental activities or exercises that will help it get into great shape and stay there. And what better way to exercise your mind than to have fun while doing it? Some of the best games for developing your critical thinking skills include Sudoku, crossword puzzles, Rubik's Cube and solitaire!

Meditate

Meditation helps your mind rest by allowing it to escape from distractions and helps you develop your critical thinking skills by stimulating:
- Alpha brain waves, which help improve logical thinking, and lets you think about and keep large amounts of information in your mind;
- Theta brain waves, which help enhance your creativity and hastens the rate at which you can solve or address daily challenges; and

- Delta brain waves, which help you achieve dreamless sleep, which is crucial for helping your tired brain rest, recover, and be rejuvenated!

A simple exercise you can do for 10 minutes a day is called the box-breathing technique, which was popularized by bestselling author Mark Divine. Sit comfortably upright with your hands on your lap. Close your eyes. Breath in for 5 seconds, hold it for 5 seconds, exhale through your nose for 5 seconds, and wait for another 5 seconds before repeating the cycle. Do this for 10 minutes every day at the minimum.

Use Parkinson's Law

Parkinson's Law states that a task's perceived importance increases as you lessen the time in which to complete it. The more you perceive a task to be very important, the more you'll be able to focus on what's important and ignore the fluff. When you're able to do that, not only will you be able to finish a task earlier, but you'll do a much better job completing it because you'll be able to focus on only the essential elements of a task.

So how do you use Parkinson's Law to help you learn how to focus better and in the process, develop your critical thinking skills even more? Give yourself shorter deadlines for finishing tasks. If you're given 3 days to submit your report to your boss, give yourself 2 days only. If you have 1 day to finish a blog entry, complete it in half a day. By giving yourself less time, you'll train your brain to work more efficiently and in a more focused manner.

Debates

You can develop your critical thinking skills by joining debates or a debate club. Preparing for a debate alone can give your mind all the workouts it needs to be able to learn how to think more critically. You see, you'll need to see things from your and your opponents' perspectives in order to maximize your chances of winning debates. If you only consider one perspective or angle, you won't be able to do well, particularly in terms of attacking the arguments of your opponents and defending your own. Joining regular debates help keep your mind sharp and trained to see all possible angles and loopholes in your and your opponents' arguments, which are all essential components of critical thinking.

Other Non-Mental Stuff

While critical thinking is mostly a matter of training your brain, it doesn't mean it's all about mental stuff. In order for you to develop your critical thinking skills, you'll need to make sure your brain is in great physical health too. And to for that, there are 3 things you'll need to consider.

Diet

No, I'm not talking about crash or fad diets for weight loss. I'm talking about what you eat on a regular basis and how it affects your mental and cognitive performance.

Eating for optimal mental performance and brain health isn't rocket science. You don't have to count calories and stuff. All you need to focus on are meal frequency and types of food.

For meal frequency, it's best to eat smaller, more frequent meals. And by this, I mean eat a small meal every 3 hours, even if you're not yet hungry. Why? This will ensure your blood sugar levels are stable, which will help you feel more energetic, alert, and focused. If you go for too long without eating, say eating only 3 huge meals thrice a day, your blood sugar can drop so low, which can lead to 2 bad things. One is lethargy and inability to focus. The second thing is binge eating, which can make you feel alive, alert, awake, and enthusiastic for the next few minutes before you start crashing back down to earth when your blood sugar drops.

For types of food, you must stick to natural, whole foods. What are these? These are real food that still resembles their original form of grilled chicken breast, brown rice, salads, fruits, and the like. Avoid processed and high sugar foods. Not only are they bad for your health, but they're also bad for your mental and cognitive performance.

Each of your small meals should be made up of a good complex carb and lean protein. Good complex carbs that won't destabilize your blood sugar include brown rice, quinoa, green leafy veggies, and sweet potatoes - in moderate amounts only of course.

Sleep

Sleep is another crucial factor that can help you optimize your brain's health, which is one of the foundations for your ability to think critically. There are 2 things you'll need to know about quality sleep: quantity (hours) and quality (depth). Let's take a look at quantity first.

How many hours of sleep do you really need? Is it 8, 7, or 9 hours? Contrary to popular opinion, 8 hours isn't really a rule but more of a guideline - a starting point so to speak. Some people get by with less while some require more. So how do you know how much do you need?

Journal your sleeping experience for the next 7 days, i.e., write down every day what times you slept and woke up, how many hours you slept, and how you generally the day after. On the 8th day, read your journal entries and you'll see a pattern, which will tell you more or less how much sleep you need every night.

The next characteristic of your sleep that you'll need to pay attention to is quality. And by quality, I mean sleep cycles and depth. Let's tackle sleep cycles first.

According to researches conduct by many sleep experts, the average sleep cycle lasts for about 90 minutes give or take. One of the ways to wake up feeling more refreshed is to time your waking up to coincide with the end of a sleep cycle, i.e., 1.5, 3, 4.5, 6, 7.5, or 9 hours after you go to bed. If you wake up in between cycles, your body and mind will be "jerked" into waking up, which will make you feel as if you hadn't slept at all. It can make you feel lethargic and sleepy the whole day. So set your alarm 6, 7.5, or 9 hours after hitting the sack and not in between.

Depth of sleep has to do with brain waves. In this case, your brain needs to register delta waves to get into deep sleep. Without getting too technical about it, one of the ways you can optimize your brain's ability to get into a deep sleep during the night is playing a delta wave soundtrack in the background as you sleep. This gives your brain a pattern to follow, which is delta, for achieving deep sleep.

Regular Exercise

Finally, getting regular exercise is one of the best ways to keep your brain in the best possible health. How? The right kind of exercise will not only help you relieve stress but also help your heart and lungs bring much needed nutrients and oxygen to your brain cells. And speaking of the right kind of exercise, what is the best type of exercise for brain health?

Aerobic exercise done at moderate intensity for at least 30 minutes for a minimum of 3 times per week is just what most experts recommend. Aerobic exercises - also called cardiovascular or cardio exercises - are those that train your lungs to get more oxygen into your body and strengthens your heart in order to more efficiently deliver nutrients and oxygen via the blood to all cells in your body, including your brain.

Now let's talk about exercise intensity. It refers to the amount of effort you exert when exercising. There are several ways to estimate the amount of effort you're exerting while exercising but most of them require a doctorate degree to understand and specialized equipment to estimate. Fortunately, there's a very simple but fairly accurate way to determine your exercise intensity. It's called the "talk test." And here's how to use it to determine the intensity level at which you're exercising so you can adjust accordingly if needed.

Exercise for 1 or 2 minutes. Then, try talking as if you're having a conversation with somebody. If you're able to talk normally and with no effort or strain at all as if you're catching up with a long lost pal over coffee, that's mild or light intensity. If you're talking as if you can hardly say anything and you have to literally catch your breath just to stay conscious, you're exercising at a high intensity level. If you're able to still carry a conversation but with some breathing strain, that's moderate intensity. That's the level you should go for. If your exercise intensity's light, speed up your movement, e.g., run or walk faster. If high intensity, slow it down.

So that's it! Aerobic exercise at moderate intensity for a minimum of 30 minutes straight for at least 3 times weekly. That's all you need for optimal brain health and mental and cognitive performance.

Chapter 5 - Activities/Games That Help Develop Critical Thinking Skills

In Chapter 4, I briefly mentioned playing games as a fun means by which to exercise your mind to develop your critical thinking skills. In this chapter, we'll take a look at some of the best, i.e., fun and effective, games you can play with other people to help them develop their critical thinking skills.

Saving Private Dumpty

The reason this game is called as such is Private Dumpty is Humpty Dumpty, an egg. In this game, the objective is to drop an egg from a particular height without breaking it as it falls. Each participating group or person will be given several materials that they can use to make sure that the egg won't break as it falls to the ground from the pre-determined height. They can use the items to either cushion the fall or slow it down like a parachute. This activity will force participants to look at the situation from many different perspectives, get creative and be effective, which all sounds like critical thinking if you ask me!

The News Paper Shrink

In this game, the objective is to fit as many people as possible while standing on a piece of newspaper, which is folded after each round in order to shrink. Participants will be grouped in twos and are given 1 big newspaper page on which to stand on for 10 seconds. If they are able to remain within the area of the newspaper after 10 seconds, they can proceed to the next round, where the newspaper will be folded in half. On the shrunken paper, they will be asked to stand on the now smaller area for another 10 seconds without stepping outside of it. If they do, they lose. If they successfully stand inside the newspaper for 10 seconds, they proceed to the next round, where the newspaper will be folded in half again, and so on until only one pair remains.

This activity will force the participants to look at many different ways and schemes for them to fit inside the area of the newspaper, which gets smaller and smaller with each passing round. Participants will need to think outside the box and come up with unique ideas on how they can stand together inside the area of the newspaper for 10 seconds, which becomes harder and harder as it's folded by half after every round.

Paper Towers

This one's a favorite activity of mine. Participants are divided into several groups, where each group is given the same number of sheets of scratch or newspapers of the same size. A good number is 20 sheets. Each group will be asked to build the tallest but strongest tower using nothing but the pieces of paper given to them. They must finish the tower in 10 minutes. The primary consideration is strength, followed by height.

To test the paper towers' strength, you must use a very big folder, paper, or fan to blow wind on the tower. If the tower tips over, it's game over. The tower must be able to withstand 3 strong and consecutive fans. If more than one tower survives 3 strong fans, the tallest one wins.

This game also forces the participants to think outside the box and look at all possible ways that the pieces of paper can be shaped, formed and linked together to create the strongest and tallest paper tower. That's why it's one of the best critical thinking development games around.

Download Your Free EBook – Complete Concentration

Go To - http://bit.ly/CompleteConcentration

Chapter 6 - Critical Thinking Apps

As we end this book, I'd like to share with you some high tech ways to develop your critical thinking skills: using apps. Considering that practically everyone has a smartphone already and access to the Internet's pretty much moot and academic for most people, why not use it to access and use apps that will make it even more fun and easier for you to work on building up your critical thinking skills? Here are some of the best critical thinking apps on the market today.

Online Strategy Games

Online strategy games are one of the best ways to develop one's critical thinking skills. Why? Where else can you combine fun and critical thinking? Compare thinking critically when working on case studies versus thinking critically when playing video games and you'll get my point! The thing with online strategy games is that you really have to plan like a general or an army commander to win. You won't get away with simply blasting your enemies to smithereens like in the case of shooter games. No, you'll really have to analyze and strategize, both of which involve critical thinking.

Playing online strategy games such as Civilization V or War Craft covers critical thinking skills such as collaboration, strategizing, analyzing, planning, and making or drawing conclusions. Oh, it also covers fun!

Neo K12 FlowChart Games

These games are both fun and simple, which can make it easier for you to exercise and develop your critical thinking skills. If you have kids, this is something that they'll most probably enjoy as they include cool topics such as food chains, biological life cycles, moon phases, the human anatomy, photosynthesis, and others.

You'll be shown incomplete flowcharts pertaining to the specific topic they're working on. Then, you'll have to click, drag, and drop the right or missing parts of the flowchart, which you can get from the right hand side of the screen. This game covers critical thinking skills such as information synthesis and summarizing.

Mind Meister

It's an app used for mind mapping, which you can use at home, school, or the office to develop higher levels of critical thinking. The app can help you to take notes insightfully, observe how different topics are interrelated, collaborate and engage with others, break down complicated ideas and concepts down into easier to understand and smaller chunks, and communicate your ideas and thoughts to others more clearly. This app covers critical thinking skills such as drawing conclusions, analysis, collaboration, and strategizing.

Go To - http://bit.ly/CompleteConcentration

Conclusion

Congratulations on finishing this book. At this point, you've learned what critical thinking is, why it's important, and many different ways to develop your critical thinking skills or bring them to a higher level. But learning or knowing is just half the battle - the other half is action or applying what you learned in real life. Not applying what you learned will only make your learning trivial instead of life-changing. And if you don't act on what you learned as soon as possible, you increase the risk of not applying them at all. And when you fail to apply any of the things you learned, there's absolutely no chance you'll be able to develop your critical thinking skills beyond where they are now.

When applying what you learned, don't think you'll need to apply them all or nothing at all. Start with baby steps, by applying one or two things you learned here and focus on consistently applying those for the next week or two. Once they become natural to you, add one or two more learnings. Again, you don't have to apply all, but it's important you apply at least some so that you put yourself in a position to develop your critical thinking skills. And more importantly, start as soon as possible. Procrastination kills.

Well, that's it! Here's to your critical thinking success my friend. Cheers!

References:

1. https://www.thebalance.com/critical-thinking-definition-with-examples-2063745
2. https://collegeinfogeek.com/improve-critical-thinking-skills/
3. https://www.teachthought.com/critical-thinking/48-critical-thinking-questions-any-content-area/
4. http://www.ucdoer.ie/index.php/How_to_Ask_Questions_that_Prompt_Critical_Thinking
5. https://www.teachthought.com/critical-thinking/6-critical-thinking-questions-situation/
6. https://www.thebalance.com/strengthen-critical-thinking-skills-2275911
7. http://operationmeditation.com/discover/5-essential-exercises-how-to-improve-thinking-skills/
8. https://letsreachsuccess.com/better-thinking-skills/
9. https://www.smore.com/0udr-fun-critical-thinking-activities
10. http://www.emergingedtech.com/2016/06/10-technology-tools-resources-teach-critical-thinking-skills/
11. https://globaldigitalcitizen.org/5-team-building-games-critical-thinking

www.ingramcontent.com/pod-product-compliance
Lightning Source LLC
Chambersburg PA
CBHW051855250726
48659CB00006B/2212